FranklinCovey™

Loving Reminders™

teen to teen

60 cool tear-out notes to send your friends!

Also available, *Loving Reminders for kids,*
Loving Reminders for couples, and *Loving Reminders for families.*

FranklinCovey.

Special Acknowledgments:

Conceived and developed by Cheryl Kerzner
Designed and illustrated by Kim Mann
Written by Sunny Larson and Debra Harris

Have you ever had a day where everything was going bad and you felt totally depressed? And then suddenly, out of nowhere, someone said something nice and it turned your whole day around? Sometimes the smallest things—a hello, a smile, a compliment, a hug, a kind note—can make such a big difference. As author Mark Twain put it, "I can live three months on a good compliment."

In my book *The 7 Habits of Highly Effective Teens*, I use a term I call the Relationship Bank Account. It represents the amount of trust and love you have in your relationship with another person. Like a checking account at a bank, you can make deposits and improve the relationship or take withdrawals and weaken it.

This little book was developed to help you make "deposits" into the key relationships of your life. So have fun with it. Use a *Loving Reminder* to say you're sorry, give out a compliment, congratulate, or express the feelings of your heart. Make someone's day, and then watch how good it makes you feel in return. Remember, in relationships, the little things are the big things.

⭐ Sean Covey

◎ Turn these pages into Loving Reminders.

- Remove a message from the book. (Hey look, tear-out pages!)

- Make it personal with your own electrifying, deeply moving note.

- Fold as shown.
  (Think back to first grade art.)

- Oooh stickers in the back of the book! Use them to seal your note.

- Slip your *Loving Reminder* in a backpack, locker, or other sly spot.

Loving Reminders
teen to teen

i love hanging out with you

You're a party all by yourself!

I'll be your vet.

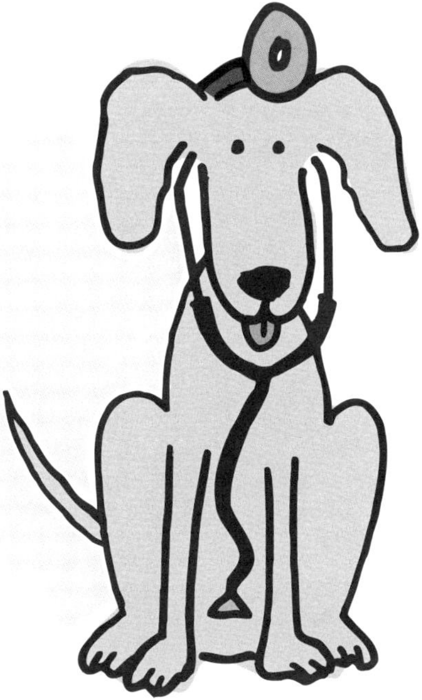

You
really
are all
that.

get psyched

We're checking out _____

at _____

from _____ until _____ !

good luck on the test

As if you need it.

  't

 2 CU

(I can't wait to see you!)

remember this?

sorry, I know what I did was lame

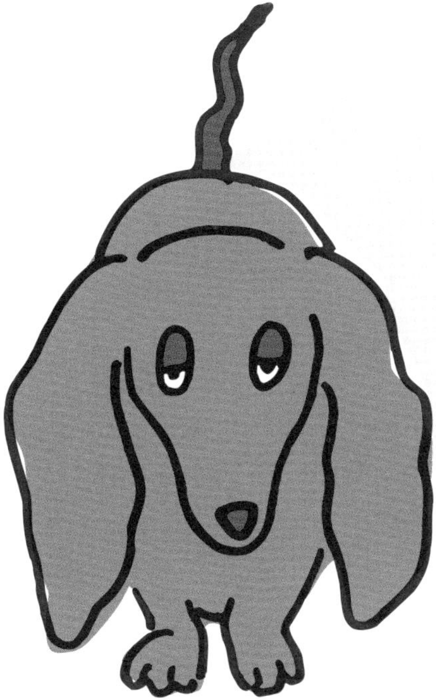

I'll never do it again.

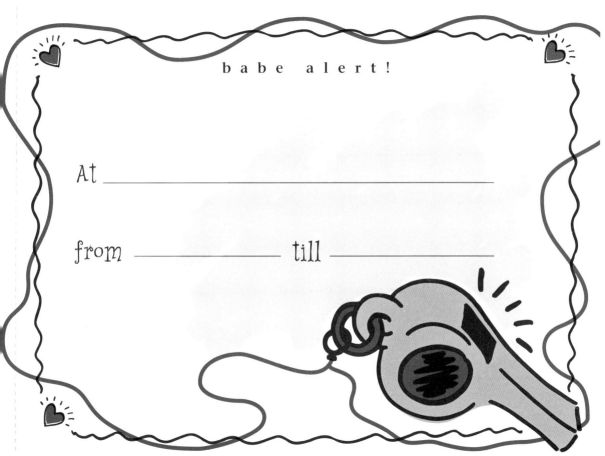

b a b e   a l e r t !

At _____

from _____ till _____

i love hanging out with you

You're a party all by yourself!

s i c k   a s   a   d o g ?

I'll be your vet.

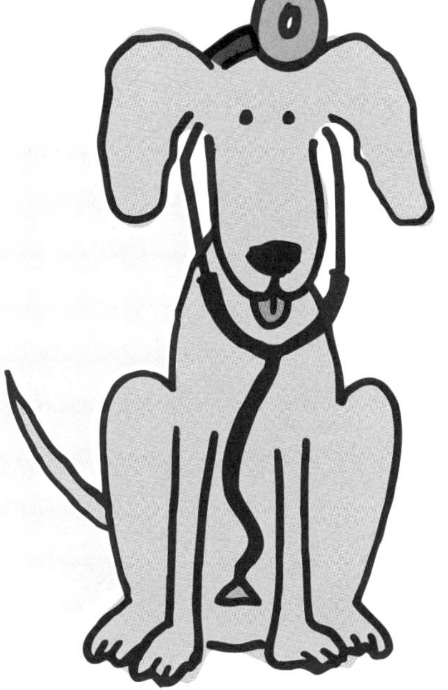

You
really
are all
that.

good luck

it!

(You can do it!)

get psyched

We're checking out _____

at _____

from _____ until _____ !

coupon

I'll be your
support for one:

☐ piercing
☐ haircut
☐ date prep
☐ other _____
(please specify)

good luck on the test

As if you need it.

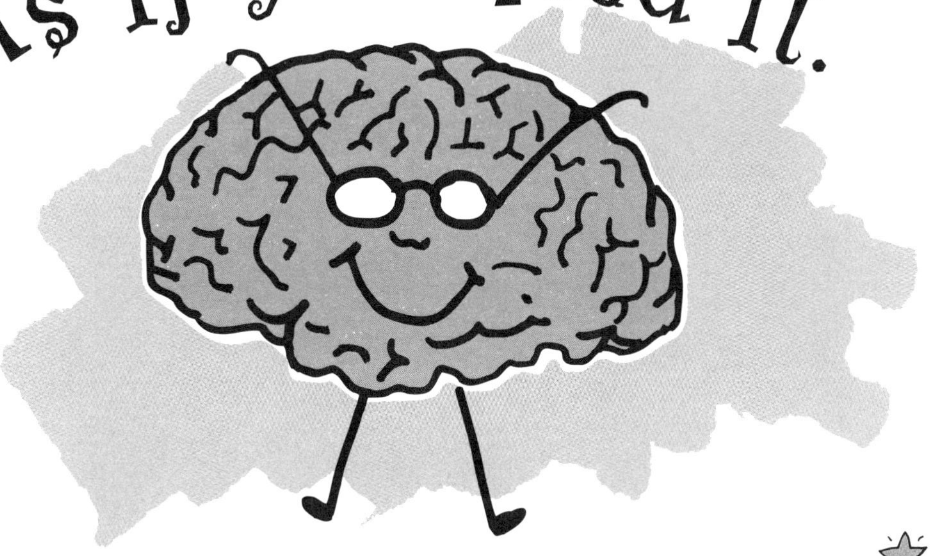

  ' t

 CU

(I can't wait to see you!)

remember this?

But then we already knew that.

babe alert!

At _____

from _____ till _____

i love hanging out with you

You're a party all by yourself!

can we talk?

I want
to patch
things up.

sick as a dog?

I'll be
your vet.

You
really
are all
that.

get psyched

We're checking out _____

at _____

★

from _____ until _____ !

big hugs

It's totally going to be okay.

good luck on the test

As if you need it.

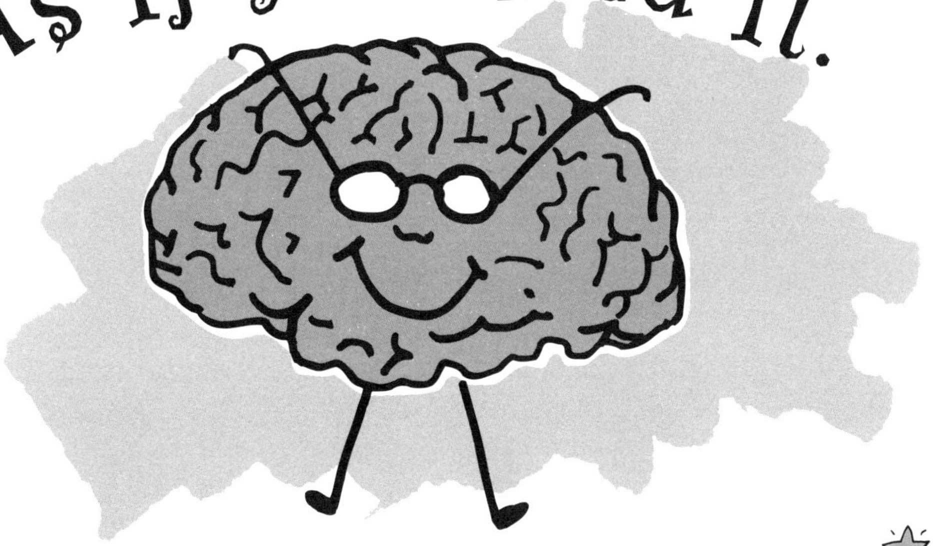

stop the madness

(I can't wait to see you!)

you rule

But then we already knew that.

b a b e   a l e r t !

At _____

from _____ till _____